He Gets The Glory From Our Story

GEANNA SIMONE

WESTBOW
PRESS®
A DIVISION OF THOMAS NELSON
& ZONDERVAN

WestBow Press books may be ordered through booksellers or by contacting:

WestBow Press
A Division of Thomas Nelson & Zondervan
1663 Liberty Drive
Bloomington, IN 47403
www.westbowpress.com
844-714-3454

Scripture taken from the King James Version of the Bible.

ISBN: 978-1-6642-5513-5 (sc)
ISBN: 978-1-6642-5515-9 (hc)
ISBN: 978-1-6642-5514-2 (e)

Library of Congress Control Number: 2022900520

Print information available on the last page.

WestBow Press rev. date: 03/21/2022

Contents

Acknowledgments

I thank you, my heavenly Father, for all your goodness. Thank you for the gift to pen my thoughts. Thank you for the unction to write this book. You are truly my way maker.

I am also grateful to the following individuals for your support and assistance during the creation of this work.

To you amazing group of survivors, who opened your hearts to me and allowed me to pen your stories. Thank you, ladies, for being so brave and transparent. I am so honored that you chose to share your life with me.

To my wonderful husband, who has supported and encouraged me, in spite of all the time it took away from you. Thank you for tolerating the lights being on. Thanks for sharing your message: "Weapons of Mass Destruction" and "His Blood, My Liquid Glory." This was your journey too.

To my brilliant, amazing daughter Ariella, thank you for my education. Thank you for all your support throughout the entire writing process, from conception to proofreading. Thank you for editing my work and for allowing me to use your sermons: "Ruth and Naomi" and "Hold on Till He Blesses You."

To my daughter Hazel, thank you for your illustrations. Thanks for the early morning talks. You are one beautiful, talented young lady and an excellent illustrator!

Last but certainly not least, to my mother: I love you, Mom! I'm so happy you are here to see my dream come to fruition. Thank you for guaranteeing me that there is nothing that I cannot accomplish. Thank you for migrating to the United States. "You were right, Mom!" "With God all things are possible."

Foreword

Wow! What a wonderful child of God. Jennifer is a true gift from God. She is a soldier of love. Jennifer is a master of words and a gift to her profession. This book is a combination of both. Oftentimes we walk the earth plane wearing a mask. Jennifer has the spiritual strength to remove the mask and disarm people in the most loving manner. Her ability to disarm people on a spiritual level brings about healing to a person's inner soul.

Jennifer's ability to share soul stories and create God's awareness is monumental. Her book is clear proof of her experience with the hearts of people. Overall, Jennifer is a woman who is committed to unconditional love. Her commitment comes through on each page of this book. The most profound part of the book reveals the heart stories of women and how life's challenges are not too big for God to handle. In the chapter "Fathers, Touch Not Your Daughters," the final comment sums it up: "Just when you think he has done too much, Jesus does it again." And just when we think God is done with building Jennifer, he has built another chapter in her magnificent life.

Nichele Williams
School Principal

Introduction

In almost every religion, the congregants are referred to as brethren. In the Christian religion, the church is referred to as a body. This usage is based on the Bible, which states that like a body, the church has different parts. It goes on to name the parts, which include the head down to the feet. The different parts of the body work together for the good of the church.

As the different parts of the body work together for the good of every individual, so is society made of different institutions—family, education, economics, etc. (Knox and Schacht, 2008). The family is a powerful institution. It has all the ingredients for a stable society. A typical family consists of a father, a mother, and children. This family unit is necessary, because families multiply in order to create more members of society. Many families today, however, consist only of a mother and children or a father and children. Many families are missing mothers, and some fathers are just not there.

Historically, strong marriages and family commitment have been central features. This is true in all cultures.

Many women are now heading households. In 1998, 54 percent of African American households were headed by single women.

Throughout history, women have outnumbered men. That is still the case today. Mothers are working, raising families, and still finding time to pray for them.

Grandparents are also becoming the new parents. Grandmothers, especially, are playing an important role in caring for their grandchildren as they pray for them. When parents are not able to care for their children, many grandparents step in and provide homes for their families (www.family.jrank.org). Gabrielle was three days old when her mother took her to her grandmother. She explained that she was suffering from depression and could not care for her. The grandparents did not think twice; they immediately made provisions for the three-day-old baby. With the help of her daughter, that grandmother cared for Gabrielle as if she was her own.

Gabrielle remained with her grandparents through high school. She was an excellent student; she was well adjusted, she lived in a beautiful home, and she enjoyed excellent medical insurance. It is important that family members work together to promote one another's emotional stability (Knox and Schacht, 2008:25). Children need people to love them and give them a sense of belonging. That is what happened for Gabrielle. This further validates the theory that the family is not always just two parents, consisting of a mom and dad. Family is sometimes a single parent. Sometimes it's a grandparent or grandparents and other extended family members, like Gabrielle's Aunt Sarah who took most of the financial responsibility for her. Gabrielle was very much loved.

The Structural Functional Framework is the most useful approach from which to view related issues like family, marriage, and relationships. This is most useful because this framework includes everything, for not just marriage. It includes theories for the family, marriage, and relationships. Other theories do not appear to address all the related issues that affect family, marriage, and other interpersonal relationships.

Families must take care of each other. Society has failed to provide the stability that a family needs. Marriage is a perfect place for counseling of both loving partners. Knox and Schacht (2008) state that no other institution focuses on meeting the emotional needs of its members as clearly as marriage and the family. Many hospitals have neonatal units, where they care for tens of thousands of babies born prematurely. They have proven that when one hugs, touches, massages, and talks to premature infants, their survival rate is much higher. Research has shown that baby cuddling is a successful treatment for sick babies. Now baby cuddling is a real job in these hospitals. She also states that baby cuddling reduces stress and regulates breathing and heart rate—demonstrating again that family remains the ultimate, nurturing component of society.

Many prominent families take pride in their names and the way they parent their children. I once knew a man who was the father of nine children. He was a prominent man is his district. He did not have to say much to his children about their behavior. They knew what the rules were. Whenever they left for school or left the home, he simply reminded them of their name, and that of course reminded them what was expected of them. He had some of the best-behaved children in the community. "Self-fulfilling prophecy."

While he did his part in expecting the best conduct, his wife, the mother of the children, told them every day that they were awesome. She told them they could be anything they wanted to be. "Looking-glass self."

The weakness of this framework is that it states that all nontraditional structures are dysfunctional. This is not necessarily true at all. As mentioned, presidents have grown out of homes with single parents and grandparents. President Barack Obama was raised by his grandmother. Families, whether traditional or nontraditional structures, continue to be the most powerful institution in society. Clearly the family unit is of utmost importance to success and achievement. In order to accomplish such success, we must pray for, encourage, and support our families. What is the key to your achievements and success? Read the stories that follow; then you decide.

All dates are removed. Names are listed that have been redacted.

1

Fathers, Touch Not Your Daughters

Pedophiles come in all races and cultures. There may be pedophiles in your very own family. What makes a relative think that it's permissible to touch his or her child, stepchild, niece, or nephew?

Linglee was only five months old when her mother passed away. She was taken in by her maternal aunt and her husband. There were no official adoptions in 1938. Family members just acquired children. They lived in a beautiful home, equipped with a maid, and Linglee enjoyed a bedroom of her own. Her new parents owned a successful family grocery store, which was attached to their home. This enabled a comfortable lifestyle.

When Linglee was three years old, her "father" started molesting her. By the time she was four, it graduated to so much more. If Linglee had had a choice, she would have chosen to live with her mother's father. She loved her grandfather. Apparently that wasn't an option. Linglee remembers falling asleep in her bed and waking up in a room closer to that of her parents. How convenient! This man, who should have loved and protected this little girl, chose instead to molest her regularly.

When she mentioned that she didn't know how she got to a different room, her aunt decided that the ghost of her dead mother was moving her while she slept. Her uncle threatened her and told her that when little girls love their daddies that is what they do together, so she didn't tell. She often asked him why he didn't do the same thing with his biological daughters. He responded, "Those things are done in private." Linglee was quite petite in stature and still is. Looking at her now, it is easy to imagine how very tiny she must have been during her early years.

Today Linglee still knows nothing about her real mother. One family member told her that mom died from tuberculosis, while another told her that her mom died due to complications during a pregnancy. Linglee grew up believing that her aunt was her real mom, and her aunt told her that her real father did not want her. One night Linglee dreamt that her aunt blurted out, "I am not your mother!" That is when she inquired and was told that her mom passed away. The abuse continued, and Linglee suffered in silence.

Linglee was eleven years old and had just been attacked by her uncle. She wobbled downstairs, barely able to walk, and the helper asked her what was wrong. That was when she told the truth about what had been going on. The helper believed her but encouraged her to wait until after her school trip to a world-renowned tourist attraction. The helper explained to her that what he was doing was wrong and that it should have never happened. She realized that there would be an uproar in the family after the dirty secret was revealed.

Linglee decided to wait. She remembered being warned to be careful on the trip. She contemplated committing suicide while on the trip. God had other plans, however, because it did not happen.

When Linglee returned from the school trip, she exposed her uncle. Of course he denied it, and her mom believed him. They were practicing Catholics, so the priest was summoned. He agreed that she was lying. The meeting took place upstairs, privately in one of the bedrooms. All bedrooms were located upstairs. As the priest exited the stairs, Linglee remembers him giving her a very dirty look as he passed her. She remembers feeling like garbage.

From that day on, she was assigned an agonizing punishment that amounted to sheer torture. She was no longer allowed regular visits to the bathroom. She was commanded to hold her urine and bowel movements until the evening, when she was fed dinner. She was forced to remain upstairs in her bedroom. One day after Linglee went to the bathroom, she stood up and discovered an enormous amount of blood in the toilet. She was rushed to the hospital and had surgery to repair the rips and tears. Even at the hospital no one questioned why an eleven-year-old girl was obviously not a virgin. That was when the family believed that he, the uncle, was guilty of the crime he was accused of. Still no one reported him, but now the abuse stopped because he was under the watchful eye of the entire family.

One year after the revelation, her mom passed away in the hospital. Her great aunt offered to take Linglee into her home, but her uncle refused to allow her to do so. Her biological father also wanted to take his daughter into his home but was not allowed. No surprises there! Soon after her mother died, her uncle lost the family grocery store that was attached to their home. He was no longer able to afford his lavish lifestyle. He was forced to move in with his mother and other family members. Linglee felt safer among the many family members. This was a good thing because she had decided that she would kill him if he tried to rape her again. By this time she was thirteen years old. She never spoke to him again. One day as she passed him in the hallway, he slapped her across her face as hard as he could. She didn't dare say one word. Even with this continued abuse, she felt that a slap was better than another session. Beyond the shadow of a doubt, God was working on her behalf. He was making a way for her. One of his sisters loved Linglee, and Linglee confided in her that she had to get away. The aunt encouraged her to start hiding clothing and other necessities before running away. She started befriending the helpers in the family store, and they were very gracious not to reveal that they were holding her belongings.

At age sixteen Linglee gathered her very heavy bag of clothing and other belongings and ran away. She struggled to carry all she owned, but God provided a guardian angel to help her carry her heavy load. A woman approached her and offered to help her. They walked about three or four miles until they arrived at her unmarried aunt's house. Linglee remained there with her aunt. She was at peace. Her aunt taught her tailoring. She was able to design and sew her own clothing. She was cared for well, and she completed high school. Unfortunately, her aunt never paid her graduation fees, so she did not march at graduation. For some, ten dollars was an enormous amount of money in 1960. Linglee's aunt enrolled her into a commercial bookkeeping school. She completed the program and became a certified bookkeeper.

At sixteen years old, Linglee visited a church with her cousins. She believed that she became a Christian that day. She felt joy in her heart, and that joy kept her. Being a staunch Christian of another denomination, her aunt felt betrayed, neglected, and angry. This was

4

the only place where Linglee felt safe, so when her aunt demanded that she make a choice between a place to live and the church, she returned to Catholicism. Linglee was blessed to work in her career as a bookkeeper. She met her husband and fell in love at eighteen, but she still she lived with the pain of that horrible abuse. The union bore two beautiful children, whom she treasures.

When she was fifty years old, Linglee rededicated her life to God and accepted salvation through Jesus Christ. She realized one day that she was not able to refer to God as "Father." She found it virtually impossible to form a relationship with her heavenly Father because she been so badly abused by her earthly father figure. She lived her life with the secret of being damaged by her father figure for eighty-three years. Finally in 2017 when she was invited to visit a church in Jamaica, Linglee was delivered. She was able to tell her story. Linglee, a beautiful eighty-four-year-old, beamed with joy as she stated that now she enjoys her new DNA of her wonderful heavenly Father. She is an anointed woman of God, serving in her church as a newly appointed church mother. Just when you think he has done too much, Jesus does it again.

2

We've Got a Heartbeat: A story of a woman who died twice and lived to tell about it

———— ⁓⟡⟆⁓ ————

My eldest daughter just had a beautiful baby girl. We both wanted to take the time to enjoy one of our shared pastimes—shopping. After an intense session of what I like to call post-baby retail therapy (PBRT), I spotted a woman who looked very familiar. Our eyes met, and we smiled at each other. As my daughter and I waited in line to pay for our items, the woman admired my granddaughter. That's when the woman and I simultaneously realized that we knew each other. She was my supervisor at an airline where I had worked more than seventeen years earlier. As I looked into her eyes, I just *knew* she had a story. I don't know how I knew, but I knew. I shared with her that I had been writing a spiritual documentary and sharing various stories that glorify God. She marveled at the fact that I knew she had a story. She asked how I knew, and I replied, "I just do."

Jesse was a walking miracle—born once, died twice.

Jesse didn't see a problem with having platelet-rich plasma therapy. After all, one of her family members had it done with great success. The procedure offered a short recovery period, and her relative didn't have any complication, so why not?

Tears flowed down her face as she explained why she had a *new* birthday. Platelet-rich plasma (PRP) therapy was expected to relieve the aches and pains that developed in her knees; she was a former athlete. Jesse would often play tennis and racquetball and was an avid bike rider. Unfortunately, while strengthening the heart, those activities caused her knee joints to deteriorate and weaken, causing bone-on-bone pain.

Her doctor practiced in a well-renowned, upscale area. However, who would ever think for a minute that he would be so careless concerning his patient's health. The platelet-rich plasma (PRP) procedure was done on her knees bilaterally; at that time this was a revolutionary new treatment designed to resolve pain by promoting long-lasting healing of musculoskeletal conditions for patients experiencing osteoarthritis of the knee, shoulder, hip, spine, rotator cuff, etc. The two-hour therapy injection is packed with growth and healing factors; platelets initiate repair and attract the critical assistance of stem cells. Her doctor did not make any efforts to inform her of the precautions that should be taken to ensure a healthy recovery; he merely handed her a prescription for oxycodone. When she asked if it was okay to use her stairs at home, she was instructed to limit her mobility. Jesse's bedroom was located upstairs. When she asked her doctor about movement, he urged her to remain upstairs, she did just that.

He had one duty. He was expected to be committed to the well-being of his patient and responsible enough to be there for her. That said, he failed to administer basic medical care such as prescribing a blood thinner. He failed to instruct her not to remain sedentary and did not advise her to consistently wear compression stockings or hose. These items are highly recommended and are required for post-surgery patients. These prevent the onset of lethal blood clots.

Just a couple of days after her PRP procedure, Jesse's son decided to pay her a visit. As he entered her upstairs bedroom, she asked him to assist her to the bathroom. When he exited the bedroom, both he and Jesse's husband heard a loud thump. To their utter dismay, that loud thump turned out to be Jesse falling. Upon finding her on the floor, immediately her husband started applying cold compresses to her neck and forehead, thinking she'd fainted. Her son called EMS, and they arrived within four minutes to find her showing signs of shortness of breath and stating "I can't breathe." She suffered her first ever cardiac and respiratory arrest with no pulse. Shortly, while she was being transported to the hospital in what would have been a "dead on arrival" (DOA) situation, God used the paramedics to perform a brief period of CPR; they resuscitated and intubated her.

Once she arrived at Aventura Hospital, she suffered a second cardiac arrest due to a bilateral blood clot. She was admitted to the intensive care unit with postcardiac arrest, bilateral pulmonary embolism, status post TPA and given IV Heparin and GI prophylaxis (to prevent any further GI bleeding). After Jesse's evaluation it was confirmed by her medical team that she had pulmonary emboli in the right lower lobe, interlobar as well the right main pulmonary artery, resulting from a bilateral blood clot that had broken in half, giving her two isolated cardiac arrests.

Jesse's condition was listed as critical for several days. Immediately she was placed in a medically induced coma, so that her team of doctors could strategize a plan of action. On day three of her eight-day stay in ICU, she underwent an inferior vena cava (IVC) filter procedure. This small filter is designed to capture any future embolism (blood clot) that might travel from her legs to her heart and lungs. On the ninth day Jesse's condition had stabilized, and she was transferred to the telemetry unit.

While preparing to leave ICU, she noticed that many ICU staff stopped by to say goodbye; some just stopped in the room to wish her well. Confused at the commotion, she asked the attending nurse who was moving her bed why so many people had stopped by to see her. She was told that many people in the unit thought of her as an ICU celebrity ... a "miracle patient." It was explained that many people do not survive the condition she experienced, especially a bilateral clot. Jesse softly told her of the grace and mercy of "her God" and the "tsunami of prayers" that was sent forward for her from her church family, coworkers, and a host of family and friends. On the tenth day, Jesse was discharged and transported via ambulance to a skilled nursing facility on day ten, which was no coincidence.

Rehab

After such a horrible ordeal, Jesse's wish was to be placed in a skilled facility for rehabilitation. She needed to receive the best possible follow-up care. She drafted a letter to her insurance company to state her wishes. Before she could forward the letter to them, her doctor arrived with the news she desired to hear. "You'll be going to the desired rehab." Jesse knew this was a divine intervention.

She arrived at the facility on a Tuesday evening, with a chest very badly bruised due to the efforts to save her life. She wore the wounds of a warrior. The staff was very kind and very caring. Jesse's roommate was a chronic complainer, and Jesse yearned to be moved and placed near a window; soon she was offered another room with a bed by the window. She spent hours gazing out her room's window, amazed at God's grace and mercy.

Her doctor recorded her condition as "medically critical" for *forty minutes.* It had been uncertain whether she would survive the bilateral clot (pulmonary emboli) that weakened her lungs and heart. But through this critical time she experienced and saw the *wonder of God's hands.* Jesse was the marvel of the staff at the rehab facility. They considered her a celebrity. Few people die and live to tell about it.

Jesse had lost core strength, having lain down for ten days. She was prescribed two separate therapies: projected mobility walk, and aquatic electric stimulation. She also received occupational therapy, the neuromuscular reeducation. She remembers talking to God on many occasions about restrengthening her. "I wanted him to give me my strength back." Jesse stated that on days when she complained, her therapist reminded her to look around the facility and take notice that she was the youngest patient there. That's when Jesse came to herself, got up, and walked. Today, Jesse's strong faith in God is encouraging and amazing. That tsunami of prayers worked.

3

Second Chances

On the day of the shower, Tanisha's baby was already dead inside of her. She had no idea. Imagine walking around with your baby dead inside of you for over a week and having no idea.

Although Tanisha was the product of a teen pregnancy herself, she didn't dare tell her mother that she was now also pregnant at sixteen. As a result, she kept her pregnancy a secret. Her boyfriend, also sixteen, demanded that she have an abortion. The Christian religion does not believe in abortion, and although she was not living a Christian life at the time, Tanisha did not feel right about an abortion.

She continued to beseech the baby's father to stay in her life and did many embarrassing things in an effort to prove that she loved him. That was what he required of her. With retching after every meal, she lost a lot of weight and was able to conceal her not so growing tummy until her sixth month. Mom finally figured it out. She was devastated. She certainly wanted better for her beautiful daughter. Her grandmother was even more disappointed; she cursed

Tanisha and forbade her to enter her home ever again. Grandma was eighteen when she gave birth to Tanisha's mother. She actually started the trend.

With much shame and embarrassment, Tanisha continued to attend high school, sometimes with a ride from her boyfriend and sometimes via the bus. Mom had many responsibilities as a single mom of three. Tanisha had two sources of support during this time: a platonic male friend from church and one of her teachers. Her teacher seemed to be very caring and expressed great concern for Tanisha. During the entire pregnancy, the baby's father wanted absolutely nothing to do with Tanisha or her baby.

With much encouragement and support from her platonic male friend from church, Tanisha rededicated her life back to God. It had now been two months since the revelation of her pregnancy. With no proper prenatal care and no proper nutrition, Tanisha was carrying a sick baby inside of her. Now, when she was eight months pregnant, her mom planned a shower for her on Saturday, December 6. Showers are a great way to be blessed with much of what is needed for the new baby. The baby girl, already named Nickesha, was blessed with many beautiful, necessary gifts. The only items that were still needed were a bathtub, baby detergent, and olive oil. Mom, now on board, instructed Tanisha to go to the mall on Monday after school to retrieve these items.

When Tanisha arrived at school on Monday, her very caring teacher expressed concern over the look of her tummy. She thought it looked different. The very young, naïve mother-to-be responded, "Everything is fine." She continued to explain, "I had my baby shower on Saturday and everything." Her teacher insisted that Tanisha should have her mom take her to the doctor as soon as possible.

When she was checked, there was no fetal heartbeat. It was determined that Nickesha was dead. The baby had passed away inside of her. The doctor was very reluctant to continue to treat her since there was a problem with her Medicaid insurance. He advised the family that they needed to work out their insurance issues or that would be the last time he would be seeing her. As she lay there, Tanisha explained, it was like an "out of body experience." She could hear them say words like *C-section*. Her aunt, who accompanied them on the doctor's visit, insisted, "No C-section!" They decided that she would carry the dead baby around until whenever she went into labor.

The doctor warned them not to go to the hospital next door, since it was a private hospital, and he would be forced to treat her. After all, she could not pay them. He instructed them to take her to a public hospital whenever she started experiencing the onset of labor. During that time, whenever Tanisha was asked about her baby's gender, she would just respond, "A girl!" She found it extremely difficult to discuss the fact that her baby was dead inside of her. She made a decision not to allow the baby's father back into her life, even with much pleading.

Tanisha also made a decision to rededicate her life to God, and she was able to let the father go emotionally and physically. She was pleased, however, that her baby's father invited her to accompany him on an errand. On their way, her water broke, and because they were closer to the private hospital, that was exactly where she was taken. Labor now becoming stronger and stronger, the nurse desperately tried to reach her doctor. He never responded. Tanisha went through the entire labor process with the nurse attempting to reach her doctor. He never came. Finally, Nickesha's lifeless body appeared. That was when her doctor walked in, angrily cut the umbilical cord and, without a word said, walked out. He was enraged.

The nurse cleaned up her dead baby, wrapped her and laid her on Tanisha's chest. She can still remember the scent of death. "It was like burnt rubber!" They left her there to bond with her dead baby. She wondered why they would leave her for so long with a dead baby lying on her chest.

Regardless of the circumstances under which our children are conceived, they are loved. Even now, seventeen years later, there are tears in Tanisha's eyes as she speaks of her little Nickesha. Ironically, the baby's father was distraught over the loss of their baby girl. He joined the navy, but before he left, he made another attempt to win Tanisha back. She explained to him that she had rededicated her life to the Lord and was no longer interested in a relationship with him. With that, he left. He wrote many letters which were left unopened. When he came home for holidays, he continued to pursue Tanisha. She stood strong; the answer was no. On one holiday he attempted suicide. He threatened that if she wouldn't come back to him, he would try it again. Tanisha insisted, "I'm never coming back to you!"

The Second Chance

It was not a long courtship. Tanisha's platonic male friend from church fell in love with her, and she fell in love with him. Not knowing that she was seeking the Lord about him, he was seeking the Lord about her. They were married soon after, and their first son together was born on the same date as baby Nickesha. God is truly a God of second chances. Now a teenager, this wonderful young man is one of the most awesome Christian young men one could ever find. Tanisha and her wonderful husband have had two other boys. As she stated, "It was the absolute right decision."

Nickesha's father completed his tour and started to stalk Tanisha. He has made many threats toward her and her new husband. He has reminded her that he is licensed, to carry a weapon. He has even gone as far as to move into her apartment complex. When they bought a home and moved, he called to wish them well and to let her know he was watching over her. Nickesha is in heaven, resting in the bosom of Jesus. Her father told Tanisha he would have made her and her husband's life unbearable had the baby survived. He is still in the area, still carries a weapon and still threatens to kill Tanisha's husband. Tanisha and her prayer partners are ever before God, for his protection from this disgruntled ex. Tanisha and her husband recently qualified and closed for an almost four-hundred-thousand-dollar home.

Thank God for a second chance. Never be too concerned about how your story starts out. What is important is how it ends. Celebrate your hard times. Celebrate your story. In tragic situations and tragedy, God is at work. He allowed it. Never be ashamed to share your story. It is a testimonial of where you've been and what you've been through. Your story helps you get your deliverance. It doesn't predict where you end up.

4

My Miracle Princess Now Looks Through God's Eyes

Who would expect to have a fourteen-month-old diagnosed with retinoblastoma? I remember it like it was yesterday. I looked into my little princess's eyes and saw a very transparent appearance in her left eye. I was not sure why, and I had never seen that before. My little princess was my first and only child, so I had no prior experience. I was very anxious to find out why her eye might look that way, so I went straight to the World Wide Web. I found information that I did not want to ever pair with my child. It stated that it could be an eye disease known as retinoblastoma. Basically, she could have cancer of the eye.

I was distraught. It is often said that one should never go to the internet to research medical information, because it will be sure to disconcert you. Well, I was very disconcerted. Due to the look of my baby's eye, I believed everything I read. I was completely rattled, but I made an appointment immediately at the eye doctor. It was confirmed: They diagnosed my little princess with retinoblastoma. I was really terrified.

An arduous journey began. The surgery was performed at a local hospital. It was a tedious journey. The appointments were many. It was unbelievable! Thank God for my sister, who was my driver and strong source of support during that time of excruciating emotional pain. This support was not always the case with my sister, so God be praised. How could my baby of only four months have cancer? But she did. My little princess indeed had cancer of the eye. I felt as though I would go insane. My body was numb to the core.

I immediately went to my pastors, who were extremely supportive, both emotionally and with prayers. They started a fundraiser to assist me with the medical cost, which was astronomical. It became very overwhelming. Feeling very bewildered, I just leaned on my church and my family. Thank God I was blessed with an amazing husband who stood by me and stood with me. I had not yet fully surrendered my life to the Lord, but I spoke to him in my heart, I could not verbalize one word. I felt such anguish at the thought of my baby wearing a prosthetic eye. An even worse feeling was the thought of her having to endure that type of surgery. I experienced miserable days and sleepless nights. That was worse! When I lay down to sleep, sleep vanished from me.

After the surgery, my miracle princess had to endure one round of chemotherapy. She had to remain in the hospital for one full week. During this process, my faith in God was strengthened. I truly learned how to trust in God. That is when I realized that trust is not just faith in action, but trust is on-the-job training. Although my husband was not yet a believer, he was kind, supportive, and loving, the kind of husband that many wives dream of. We continued being the nurturing loving parents we always were.

I gathered strength from the encouragements of my church. Their optimism helped us become more optimistic. We are very blessed to have them in our lives. My miracle princess's illness not only drew me closer to God, but it taught me that I was not a victim but an overcomer. Because of her illness, I developed more sympathy for others, and I became more appreciative for the prayers of the righteous. As I mentioned previously, during this process, I could not verbalize my prayers. I did know that prayer required perseverance. I was so distracted with appointments, I really leaned on my church. What a relief to have pastors and members with such faith in God.

So many times, as young people, we consider ourselves invincible, but soon we realize that we are but flesh. and mere humans. Today my princess's walk is strengthened, my faith has been renewed, and my miracle princess is healed. I know that God is able. When I focused on the problem, I became overwhelmed. Now I realize that there is purpose in all our experiences. I know that my God is able to do just what his word promises. I have vowed to be obedient to his word, trust in him, and continue to see miracles in my life. I can now encourage others to fix their eyes on the way maker, when there seems to be no way. He is the way maker, the miracle worker, and our deliverer.

5

Bullied, Used, and Abused; But God

———— ✵ ————

Low self-esteem: What is this debilitating disease? It is as serious as heart disease and cancer. This disease exists when someone has a feeling of insignificance or a lack of importance. Persons with low self-esteem also have no self-worth and lack self-confidence. Most times it's after one overcomes low self-esteem that they realize they had it. Psychologists are still researching the reason for low self-esteem. Low self-esteem doesn't care who you are, how beautiful you are, how educated you are, or how much money your family has. What causes low self-esteem?

To look at Laura, it was difficult to imagine that this beautiful, intelligent young woman lacked self-worth. It is absolutely fine to teach your children not to esteem themselves higher than others. On the other hand, they must be taught that it is okay to have high self-esteem and see themselves as just as important as others. Laura's mother taught her children that they should be seen and not heard. She taught her daughter not to be overly proud, so it took Laura practically all her life to speak up about anything or to be proud of herself and her accomplishments.

With the exception of Laura and her mother, no one knew that Laura was being bullied by her so-called friend who attended the same church and the same school. Yes! They attended the same church and the same school. Her "friend," Tamara, competed in the same competitions—singing, modeling, or anything that Laura did. When Laura entered a modeling competition, Tamara of course entered as well. Laura won by unanimous decision. Laura was the winner, hands down, but when they returned Monday morning, the story told at school was that Tamara had won, and Laura was sure to be jealous. Nothing could be further from the truth. Laura won the other two competitions as well. Tamara's family started a rumor that Laura's family had the competition fixed.

There came a time when Laura's family suffered a horrific tragedy: Laura's uncle was shot near his home. It is believed that he was assassinated by a rival boyfriend of his ex-girlfriend. Her uncle's fingerprints were the only ones on the weapon, so they ruled it suicide. Tamara could not wait to return to school to announce that Laura's uncle had killed himself. Tamara had a group of other girls who assisted her as she incessantly taunted her friend Laura. Laura's mother declared to Laura that God would work it out. Tamara was so very guileful with her bullying that it was difficult to detect. She had a soft, sweet voice and an angelic face, but she was a bully. She had many people fooled. Laura's mother wasn't a pushover and would have given her life for her children, but most times Laura said nothing. And when she did, she begged her mother not to respond for fear of any repercussions.

Intent on making Laura's life a nightmare, Tamara did not know that Laura was suffering from a lot more. She had been experiencing inappropriate touches and abuse from a very young age. Her low self-esteem was a result of feelings of worthlessness, loneliness, and mistrust. Tamara didn't care that they were young church sisters or that Laura looked up to her. She played on what she perceived to be Laura's weakness.

Laura's upbringing was one that many like her share worldwide. Her parents divorced while she was still in grade school. Her mother, Angelina, struggled to make ends meet. Laura's father never played a role in their lives. Even prior to the divorce, he was hardly ever around. The limited resources forced Angelina to leave Laura and her siblings with a family member. He was the one at whose hands Laura was abused. Laura never felt true love from a man. Her father had abandoned the family. She sought true love and acceptance from the first man who should have loved her the most, her father. However, like so many, he was nowhere to be found.

Still, life went on, and her mother made it her primary goal to create a good life for her children. Laura excelled in school. Trying to put the past behind her, she was heavily involved in her church activities after graduation. She had no idea of what to do. Although ambitious, Laura did not come from a line of educated people, just hard workers trying to make it. She had no guidance, no one to offer any insight.

Sadly, her church family did not offer any support. In fact, the pastor's family was the worst at counter-motivation that she had ever seen. Each person took their time to taunt and harass her about going to college. They thought that she was wasting time with life and used every opportunity to ask her about her educational plans.

Granted, Laura dreamed of going to college, but it seemed like a goal very far out of reach.

So Laura tried to find her way. She worked various jobs. She even tried her hand at personal training and fitness, but she got so much attention because of her taut physique that she found it an uncomfortable career choice. That was when she decided to find a stable position at a Fortune 300 company and settle in.

At age twenty, Laura started to spend time with Dean, a very experienced, handsome forty-two-year-old man who had just completed a twenty-year enlistment in the military. Being twenty-two years her senior, Dean was able to convince Laura that she would one day be his wife. Laura kept spending time with him. She believed in his lies. Dean's family was very familiar with Laura's family, as they grew up together and attended the same church. Dean was already an adult of legal drinking age when Laura was born.

Time passed, and Laura spent more time with Dean, all while being ridiculed and disrespected by his family. His women relatives seemed to be jealous of this much younger, beautiful woman entering their family circle. After all, Dean and his siblings had been raised with the belief that they were better than everyone else in every way imaginable, from smarts, to looks, to wit. This could not be further from the truth. Yet they used it as a point of bullying those around them, including Laura. Every family event was another opportunity for Dean's family to disrespect Laura.

As if it weren't enough for Dean's family to be so mean-spirited toward her, Laura discovered that Dean was a compulsive liar and womanizer, cheating on her with numerous women. She often found evidence, things like movie tickets, condoms, and women's personal items. He would say that his daughter had friends over and must have left those items there unbeknownst to him. Low self-esteem made her want to believe his lies. She even caught him with women. He explained them away as coworkers.

Many would ask why Laura chose to stay in such a demeaning relationship. It would take years for her to be able to answer that question. For years, when Laura would threaten to break up with Dean (or actually do so), he would threaten her life. He would threaten to assassinate her character. She couldn't have that. Plus, she genuinely cared about him. He used his wits and years of experience to attempt to outsmart her. What Laura discovered through counseling, prayer, and mediation, was that she had never dealt with past childhood issues, from being abandoned by her father to being molested by her relative. The betrayal she felt caused her to gravitate to those who did not value her.

One day, Laura heard a gospel message that changed her life. As a result of this message, she began to get a little more courage and a little more focus. Already working a full-time job, Laura began to take a few more college courses. She started to delve into her singing and songwriting. As a beautiful and talented young woman, she constantly had entertainers and record label executives interested in her work. Still, Laura made time to finish her studies. She went on to finish her bachelor's degree and then a master's degree as well.

As Laura worked through her studies, she started to make decisions that spelled the start of the end of her dead-end relationship. She purchased a home. She became more open to meeting new people. During this process, she formed a music group, with mostly family members. One of the musicians took a particular interest in Laura. Turns out that they actually had history. He was longtime friends with her brother, and she with his brother.

Laura eventually ended that relationship and went on into another. This time, she was determined not to waste time as she once did. She found herself engulfed in her career and her doctoral studies, when she proverbially looked around and saw that, as before, this new relationship was filled with lies and suspicions. Determined not to let history repeat itself in this manner, Laura exited. This time she was ready for more. She wanted marriage. She wanted a family. She wanted to be serious in her walk with God. That was when she also began to realize her self-worth. She finally identified with Proverbs 31, wherein her price is far above rubies.

Through it all, Laura was motivated to better herself. There were times when she thought she was wasting time, but she later realized that she actually accomplished a lot during those trying times. She also discovered that when she felt alone, Christ was there. She had a circle of friends who supported her. Her mother and grandmother had been praying all along. But most of all, God had favored her. Although she might have felt abandoned, she was never by herself. She was actually very sheltered and surrounded.

Laura reconnected with her family friend—the group member from years before. Today, Laura is married to this man, who was there all along. He was in love with Laura for as long as he could remember. Their connections ran even deeper than either of them realized. They had in fact lived right around the corner from each other since grade school. They even attended the same elementary, middle, and high schools. Their families were friends for years. Laura finally identified with God's providence in her life, and when she did, they were engaged within six months and married in a year. They have a beautiful baby and a gorgeous home that Laura always desired. Her dreams have come true.

Life is just starting for Laura. She is an example that prayer works. Those who mocked her for not yet having a college degree came to know that her doctoral degree was conferred upon her. She is a professional life coach and administrator. She is also a college educator and new author. Laura works in her church and is a motivator who seeks perfection in everything she does. She has allowed God to use her to come into her own as a mother, wife, daughter, and woman. Laura is a twenty-first-century force to be reckoned with. She is a prime symbol who reminds people that your start does not determine your end.

6

Shaken but Not Broken

The Days have certainly seen their share of nights. Now that they have been enlightened, they are using their days to inspire and enlighten others.

Shakinah always looked older than her age. She was the second of nine children, and her mom relied on her to help babysit her younger siblings. Because of these responsibilities, she acted older than her age as well. She was expected to bathe, dress, feed, and watch over them. Even now as adults, some of her siblings are still telling the stories of Shakinah tattling to their parents of their wrongdoings.

Although she was a bright girl, she was very shy and always felt afraid of loss. She would often have dreams of her mother dying. It was an ongoing fear because her father appeared very mean, or so she thought; he often yelled, and never spared the rod. Shakinah journaled her feelings, always carrying a pen and paper. Persons she came in contact with often asked if she was a teacher.

Having no clue what her purpose was, she sought to be a flight attendant, or an airline ground attendant. Most parents in the

Caribbean feel that if they tell their daughters they are pretty, it may go to their heads and cause them to misbehave. She was never told she was pretty, so she felt that this career would give her a sense of validation. Fifty years ago, that was a well sought- after career.

Shakinah migrated to the United States with her family soon after middle school. She states that she had never seen such clean, beautiful streets. Four children followed in May 1969, and the other four would be arriving six months later. One child was born here in States. That first summer was awesome, because Shakinah and her siblings took advantage of the warmth to become acclimated to the culture of the United States. They often ran next door to buy pork rinds and grape sodas from the corner store, being careful to return before Dad came home from work. The corner store was their neighbor, since they themselves lived in Big Daddy's storefront. It was an unoccupied grocery store, and they were very lucky it was available. Big Daddy was every one's "Big Daddy," and he owned many properties in the area. Their parents became friends with Big Daddy's sister, so it was easy to obtain.

When summer ended, Shakinah and her siblings entered high school. In those days, people of color with no money were not really encouraged by school counselors to pursue a college education. Yet Shakinah and her older sister worked very hard in school. Her sister aspired to be a registered nurse and Shakinah a flight attendant. She was afraid to tackle geometry, algebra, or any type of formal math. No counselor encouraged or recommended it. Her parents really didn't know the difference, so she took general math. She did very well and did just fine in high school. Shakinah's sister went on to college and indeed studied nursing.

One year later, Shakinah completed high school and attended an airline school. It was unbelievable! She returned home and at first landed a job with a smaller carrier. A few years later, she landed a job with a major airline. She was very excited and was a dedicated employee. During her twenty-five years tenure, she met and married a man who promised her the life she longed for. Having been divorced once already, she was ecstatic at the thought of a godly, loving man. He seemed to love her three children, which was very important to this young mother. They were very dedicated to their church and they appeared very happy. The marriage was less than happy, however. James was often caught in adultery, but Shakinah stayed.

Eventually, she became ill and was forced to apply for disability. She attributed the illness to her tumultuous marriage. She raised children, as well as her granddaughter. As she was going through her second divorce, her daughter, having put herself through school, approached her mother with an idea. She encouraged her mom to attend college and become an educator. She went one step further and handed her mom a college application. A whole new life emerged for her. Unfortunately, in college, she studied just enough algebra to get by. In the interim, since she had enough credits to become a substitute teacher, that was exactly what she did. Little did she know that in order to become a teacher, various types of math were required.

Nevertheless, Shakinah graduated with very good grades. Her grades were so outstanding, she was invited to join the honor society. After graduation, she continued to work as a substitute teacher with hopes of passing the teacher exam and becoming a certified teacher. She was able to pass all the other areas of the exam—except math, of course. She was now at her school for approximately three years. The principal was very happy with her performance and gave her an interim teaching position.

While she operated in that position, the principal recommended a tutor. Incidentally, the tutor was the same professor who wrote the instructional manual for the math practice exam. It was very expensive but Shakinah was able to study with that instructor for eleven months. Imagine learning algebra, geometry, statistics, and probability, all within eleven months. It was no easy task but she started sitting for the exam after the eleventh month of studying. After a couple of tries, Shakinah decided not share her test date with anyone. Although her husband was very supportive, it was very disappointing to him when she failed the test. Instead she asked her daughter to be in prayer with her. There is something special about intercessory prayer. On the day of the exam, her daughter shared a vision she had on the previous night. She had a vision of her returning from the test site waving the test results in her hand. The results said *PASS*. Shakinah could not pray alone. She was too nervous. Her daughter prayed and believed with her.

Shakinah passed the exam and became a certified teacher. Thousands of people are currently in school who are not able to pass this very difficult exam. It had to be God who allowed her, an older student who had been out of school for a number of years, to pass this exam. God is real, and prayer works.

Shakinah taught school for four years, and during her fourth year, she received devastating news. She had developed breast cancer. Being a passionate praise and worship leader and an assistant pastor, she was ashamed to share such horrible news with her church. How could this happen to her? she thought. How would she tell her members to worship God no matter what, when she herself had cancer?

She decided not to share it with her entire church. One woman whom she trusted and did decide to share the news with, joked about it, saying, "At least you look cute in wigs." Not funny to someone who now had the fight for her life on her hands. Shakinah, along with her husband and daughter, called on other prayer warrior friends, who prayed and supported them. Her husband, daughter, and son-in-law, made sure she got to her appointments and supported her through the entire process.

Shakinah is cancer-free today. She continues to worship God as if it is her last day on earth and recently published her first book. She is currently working on her second book, and she gives God the glory for her deliverance and healing.

7

I Had the Weapon, I Just Had to Use It

On the day Mary's mom discovered she was living a lesbian lifestyle, she held a lexorcism (lesbian exorcism).

At the age of twelve Mary accepted the Lord as her personal Savior. She lived like most other little girls of Christian parents. If your parents are Christians, then you are taken to church, and when your parents feel that you understand, they encourage to be "saved" too. Mary didn't really understand what that meant; she just knew she was saved.

For the most part, her home life was normal, except she never really observed warmth between her parents. They appeared to have a business arrangement. They paid their portion of the bills and shared the responsibilities like a business arrangement. On the day that Mary discovered and revealed to her mother that her dad had a girlfriend, that was the day her dad stopped taking care of her. If Mom was home, then Mary had food, and her needs were met. When Mom was away, Mary suffered lack. No food or water, and she went without the everyday needs that a little girl has.

Dad ignored her and refused to communicate with her. Mom remained with Dad, and Dad continued to cheat. This ill treatment continued for five years. It was very confusing for Mary. This was supposed to be a Christian home. That was Mary's first experience with rejection. Middle school was devastating—her second experience with rejection. There she had her first crush. When the boy did not reciprocate her feelings, Mary was heartbroken. Still she pressed on and made it through to high school.

High school was where Mary fought and lost many battles. At one point, she spoke up for a friend, and that landed her in the midst of a confrontation. She was chased by a gunman who attempted to murder her. For months Mary lived in fear, looking over her shoulder. Finally, the gunman was caught and arrested. High school was also where Mary was introduced to the gay lesbian lifestyle. Mary's sister was living that lifestyle, so Mary thought, why not? That was the first time since she was twelve that she felt wanted or loved.

During that same time, Mary was blessed with a wonderful job with a major airline. Great job, yes! Wrong crowd, however. Mary was introduced to drugs and alcohol. Having her beautiful partner on her arm, a great job, and the ability to purchase drugs and alcohol, she felt validated. Little did Mary know that this relationship would prove to be insufferable. Getting little or no sleep, along with popping pills and drinking, Mary began to experience hallucinations. She also got involved in pornography. That was when Mary's mother discovered her gay-lesbian lifestyle and staged the lexorcism. The number five seemed to be a significant number for Mary, because this period of riotous living lasted five years. Mary's mother was at her wits' end. She tried everything, from threatening to praying and fasting.

One day, Mary's mother finally asked God to either fix Mary or kill her. Mary continued to experience hallucinations. Actually, they became worse. The way Mary tells it, "I felt sensations in my body and felt someone touching me constantly. It was a stronghold!" she said. One day, out of nowhere; Mary was fired from her wonderful job. I believe God was at work. She continued to be out of control. One night during one of her hallucinations, her mom realized that she was way too out of control, for her to handle at home. She could no longer handle her daughter's erratic behaviors alone.

That night, Mary was Baker Acted and placed in the mental ward at the hospital. Mary's mother continued to pray and seek God for her daughter's deliverance. After only three days, Mary was released from the hospital and returned home. Believe it or not, she went right back to the same lifestyle of drugs, alcohol, and riotous living. Not wanting to hear what her mother thought about her wrongdoings, she moved out and moved in with her lover. Mary picked right up where she left off. Having no job, a drug and alcohol problem and a partner to take care of, Mary started panhandling.

Soon after moving in with her partner, she discovered that her partner was pregnant. "Wow!" What a disappointment, she was rejected again, but she stayed, just as she saw her mother do. She now had a bigger family to care for. Panhandling was not earning enough, so they got evicted.

Mary was arguably the kindest woman of all time. As they bounced from hotel to hotel, literally living one day at a time, Mary started hearing voices. This time the voices were telling her to give up and try it God's way. That day, Mary started seeing miracles. God's goodness and faithfulness were extended to her; even in her waywardness and disobedience, God was still providing for her.

One night, Mary dreamt that she was engaged in an argument with her partner. She told her partner that she wished she had never met her. Mary started praying. She stopped drinking, stopped smoking marijuana, and stopped taking pills. The stronghold of pornography was broken, and Mary no long had desires for her partner. When Mary made a decision to change, and prayed; she was delivered. Second Chronicles 7:14 states: If my people which are called by my name, would humble themselves and pray, and seek my face, and turn from their evil ways; then will I hear from heaven, I will forgive their sin and heal their land.

Mary started understanding her authority to use the weapons of mass destruction. Mary rededicated her life to the Lord. She fasted, prayed, read her Bible, and started praising and worshipping God. Mary, who has never been with a man, is believing God for a godly husband and a house full of children.

God did it again!

8

Case Closed

Jill knew she was in trouble when her children's grandmother showed up at her house that fateful day one summer. She (the grandmother) took one look at her teenage grandson and demanded that he come with her. Within an hour, the boy's mother had to call his grandmother back and ask her to return to get the baby as well. DCF was there, and it was either grandma or a foster home.

It was rumored that Jill was using drugs and exposing herself while neglecting her minor children. DCF was called, and Mom was drug tested on site and tested positive for cocaine, while breastfeeding her baby. This would prove to be a very long journey for Jill and her children. This was not the first time Jill's mother had to remove her grandson from his home.

Jill and her children's father had a very volatile relationship filled with physical fights and drug abuse. They were both aggressive toward each other, but they both remained in the home they shared. The family prayed for them both. They shared that they asked God to either fix them or separate them. Jill's boyfriend's family was convinced that she was the rabble-rouser in the relationship. She swears that her boyfriend was a sneaky drug abuser who was very duplicitous. This dysfunctional relationship continued for over thirteen years.

During this entire time, Jill's boyfriend was a faithful guitar player in church. He also cleaned the church faithfully every week. Jill never attended church there. Jill's mother did not take her children to church as a young mother. However, prior to passing away, her mother started attending church with her grandchildren's father. When Jill lost her mother in a tragic car crash, things got worse between her and the boyfriend. She was very close to her mother and in fact, so was her boyfriend. Jill was devastated, and seemed to be extremely depressed. Good jobs did not come easy for them, since drug tests were always random and positive.

After the court hearing, the teenager was ordered to remain with his grandmother, and the baby was placed with his grandmother's sister. Because Dad did not report Mom, he was also charged with neglect and was not allowed to have the children without being supervised. This started a sad, petrifying journey of education attorneys, state attorneys, and child advocates. During this time, Jill's two sisters also lost their children to the state.

Jill was determined to have her children back with her at some point, so for the most part, she was at court hearings fighting for her boys. The children's father did not always attend court. He stated on many occasions that it might be a speedier process for Mom to fight for their children. During the fight, they had two more babies, one girl and one boy. They were allowed to keep those children. The family felt that Dad was not ready to give up drugs and a life of riotous living.

Twelve months passed, and one day during the thirteenth month, something miraculous happened. The children's father, Jill's boyfriend, went to church and asked his pastor to please baptize him. Of course, the pastor was ecstatic. He had been praying for this young man for years with no positive results, but he began to notice a change in his demeanor. A few months later, he was baptized. He started having negative test results, and a new chapter started for Jill and her family. Jill also started having good test results, and her boyfriend of fourteen years proposed. They were married in a small intimate ceremony.

After having had to visit their children under the watchful eyes of the state, they finally got to the place where they could see their children unsupervised. That lasted for about six months. Their oldest son, who was placed with his grandmother, swore he would never go back to live with his parents. After having unsupervised visits with his parents for a few months, he changed his mind and decided to return home. Home has changed for the better, he states. Mom and Dad are not high anymore, and they are not beating on each other anymore. Perfection has not been reached yet, however. With both parents finally able to work a regular job, the oldest son now has an abundance of responsibilities, mostly babysitting, but he doesn't seem to mind.

The younger of the two, is struggling with the transition. Transition is especially difficult for children with special needs. A miraculous thing happened during the visitation process. Rose, the caretaker of this beautiful little boy, has taught special needs children for twenty years. She is patient and kind and wants to remain in his life. His parents decided that the relationship that she shares with their son is so positive and unquestionably beneficial to him that it should continue. It is hopeful that they will live up to that promise. God most certainly moves in mysterious ways. The mother of the children has now requested baptism. The family and church family's hope and prayer is that these parents will continue to live up to their new way of life.

The younger of the two boys is still not adapting well to his return home. However, the parents are using the out-of-sight, out-of-mind strategy. The wonderful caretaker misses this child as if he was her very own. She longs to see him. When he sees her at church, he cries to go home with her. Sometimes he's allowed to. The parents are promising that as soon as he becomes acclimated again, they will allow weekend visits. She is happy that she had him in her life as long as she did. God used her as his guardian angel, and she promises to forever hold him near and dear to her heart. This entire family experienced deliverance.

9

Violated by One Man and Beaten For It by My Daddy; But God

————— ❧ —————

Destiny was almost fifteen years old when her father found a girlfriend. He ordered her mother out of their home after constant fights and beatings. Mom, unable to provide a home for herself and her five children, left the children with their father and moved into a rented room.

Destiny, being the eldest child, was commanded to take on all of the household chores. She washed, cooked, and of course tended to her three brothers and one sister. Destiny did not have the luxuries of a washer and dryer, or a microwave oven, to make things a bit easier. Everything had to be done by hand. Along with these other responsibilities, she also had to continue to complete her high school studies. She was expected to achieve and maintain good grades. Miraculously, she was able to do that. Destiny did not have much time to spare, but she remained a kind, responsible, and friendly young girl, with just a few friends, or so she thought.

One afternoon, on her way home from school, Destiny accompanied her best friend to her home with a group of their other peers. Like young girls do, the girls gathered in her friend's bedroom, talking and giggling. Suddenly a man she had never seen before walked into the room, and all the other girls ran out and left her alone. She had been set up. In spite of her screams for help, that afternoon, Destiny suffered a brutal assault. As distraught, bruised, and devastated as she was, she could not breathe a word of this horrible ordeal to anyone, especially her father. After all, Destiny would have to explain why she did not come straight home after school. She was forced to keep it all to herself.

Some things cannot be concealed however. The month that followed, Destiny did not get a period. It became very evident that something was wrong, when she had to race to the powder room every morning to regurgitate. Her dad, realizing something was very wrong, took her for a doctor's visit. When it was confirmed that she was indeed pregnant, her dad beat her practically lifeless and then had the baby aborted.

Amid all the dysfunction at home, Destiny completed high school. She missed her mother desperately, but her mom lived in only one room so there was really no space for her or her siblings. Destiny's dad gave true meaning to the saying, "Papa was a rolling stone." After fathering a daughter with his mistress, he broke up with her. Soon after that, Destiny's dad met another woman and fathered another child, a boy, and brought him into the home to add to the other siblings. Destiny had to take care of this child as well. He then married a new woman who had two daughters from a previous relationship.

Destiny's dad now visited his own children, belted out orders, beat them up when he deemed necessary, and then left again to his new home. Destiny no longer had direct access to her father. When Destiny and her siblings needed to speak to their father, they had to do so through their new stepmother. Yes! He married this new woman. That made Destiny very uncomfortable, but she had no choice.

After the rape and beating, Destiny never left home except to go to school. Two years later, at the age of eighteen, Destiny decided to take a walk. Somehow, her dad found out, met her back at home, and beat her up. Destiny remembered looking at a knife that was in reach at the time of the beating and considered stabbing her father. On that day, Destiny decided she had to leave, or she could one day murder this man.

She went to her mother, and Mom made room for her. Destiny's four brothers were now left to fend for themselves. Her sister was sent away to school in Kingston. The boys literally had to now raise themselves. Although Destiny loved and cared for her brothers, she could no longer tolerate the abuse. The four young boys were not visited by their mothers, and dad only came around to bring a little food, give his expectations, and beat them. The little food he brought only sufficed for dinners. They were expected to attend school every day. No breakfast or lunch was provided, but they attended anyway.

As if their dad wasn't far enough away, one day he announced to the boys that he was going to America. This was not really a big deal, since they were on their own anyway. When Dad sent money for his sons, he sent it to their stepmother, who shortened their portion even more. Dad then sent for his wife, their stepmother. Now their money came to their stepsisters, who were no better than their dad and stepmother. Dad built a mansion in Jamaica with the money he earned in the United States. His children were not invited there, so they continued to live on their own.

As time moved on, the children were surviving, and Dad became ill. Having worked on old buildings, he contracted asbestos-related lung cancer. Destiny remembers visiting her dad at the hospital and finding him seated on a bench in the hallway. He had been waiting on an available bed for the past three days. Understand that in Jamaica, when a patient is admitted to the hospital, they must provide their own sheets, pillows with cases, and blankets. Her father had none of these items provided for him. His new family was at home in the mansion, not visiting the man who had provided so nicely for them. They never brought him bed sheets, a pillow, or a blanket. Destiny didn't have much money, but what she had she shared with him and left. As much as he abused and neglected her and her siblings, she had compassion on him. Dad passed away soon after. He died a very sad, lonely man. Destiny remembers her grandmother's prayers for them, her grandchildren. She began repeating those prayers.

Destiny was now nineteen years old. That was when she met Gilbert. Her mother did not like him because she never saw his eyes. Gilbert never looked directly at anyone. Destiny dated him anyway. One year later, she became pregnant. That was when Gilbert showed his true colors. He gave Destiny three thousand dollars and told her to have an abortion or forget about him forever. She threw the money in his face and walked away.

She remembers reading to her unborn baby. Destiny's water broke at seven months. On that day her premature baby girl was born. Destiny states that she did not even have a blanket to wrap her newborn baby. Her mom stepped in, however, and provided clothing for her infant granddaughter. When Destiny's daughter, Faith, was four years old, she started taking her to the library. Faith soared through elementary and middle school, and having passed all necessary exams, she was able to attend a private prep school at no cost to Destiny.

After Faith finished high school, Destiny migrated to the United States. Faith passed the SAT with very high scores and attended college on a full scholarship. She also attended law school on a full scholarship. Today Faith is a practicing attorney. Destiny is still a praying mother and a licensed minister. Her only regret is that Faith's father did not live to watch her success from afar. Destiny met and married a wonderful man, Dennis, who loves and adores her. Her sister is a Christian, a registered nurse residing in another state, and oh yes!—her brothers are also Christian men who are successful in their chosen careers. Destiny's mother resides with her and her husband. Yet another example of deliverance through prayer.

God gets the glory again!

10

Pushed into My Purpose: From the Crack House to My Dream House

———— ❧ ————

She came to the United States with no green card, and no money. Like so many, she was in search of the American dream. She was blessed to live with my sister, until the day they had a really intense argument. She was soon thrown out. Looking back now, she realizes she should have humbled herself and just asked my sister to allow her to remain there.

She had a job in a restaurant, working as a server, but the job only paid $120 per week. Some weeks, she was paid $150 including tips. Her pay was not enough to afford rent for an apartment, but with no green card, she could not get a better paying job. The situation was less than good. As a matter of fact, it was terrible. She did not have many options, so she started living in a crack house. She was not a drug user, but the rent was affordable.

During that time, she did not have a personal relationship with God, but she knew of him because her grandmother had raised her in a Christian environment. She prayed for her family constantly.

She can still remember hearing her grandmother asking God to provide for her grandchildren, when they lived in that one-bedroom shack.

Sometimes God uses situations to draw us to him. The adversities tend to transform us and make us stronger. Maybe you've seen this in your own walk with the Lord or watching the Lord work in someone else' life.

If you have ever traveled on the ocean, then you know that you can't always expect smooth sailing. Life is like a journey on the ocean. There will be storms, winds, gigantic waves, fogs, icebergs, reefs, and even rocks. These possible hazards are dangerous for the traveler. We will all experience challenges and difficulties. What do we do when we face the challenges, when out on life's seas?

When the disciples found themselves involved in a storm, they woke the Savior up as he lay resting in the belly of the ship. He awoke and rebuked the waves. He was right there with them, yet they were afraid and had forgotten about his power. He later rebuked them for their lack of faith.

In life we must endure many hardships. There are times when we feel as though there's no way out. We must develop an attitude of "survival by any means necessary." This young woman ended up moving from one crack house to another. At one particular crack house, they even sold crack in the hallway. She was very private about her suffering, and she was careful not to say anything to anyone, since she was living in the United States illegally. She was ashamed of being homeless and was afraid of being thrown out of the country. She dreamed of taking a bath or a shower. To freshen up, she was compelled to use the restroom in the restaurant with the help of a foam cup, paper towels, and the toilet bowl. As poor as they were in that broken-down shack, this was much worse. She longed for normalcy or just a better life, and she knew there was hope here in America.

She had a platonic male friend who worked at the department store near her place of employment, the restaurant. He asked his brother to allow her to temporarily reside in his vacant condo. His brother agreed. She was more than ecstatic! After she moved in, he demanded rent, and the required payment was—let's just say he did not want money. She not only refused, but also informed his girlfriend. All she had was her dignity, but she held on to it. That very night he threw her out. It was not just very cold but it was raining. She sought shelter at the bus stop, and that's where she slept most of that night. When her friend found her, he picked her up, gave her a Bible, and told her God would see her through.

She held on to those encouraging words. She didn't know it then, but those words were worth more than money. Still she saw no way out. She was forced to make the crack house her home again.

One day, while working, she recognized one of her customers driving by slowly. It was the same man who had asked her for my number when he patronized the restaurant on a previous occasion. She remembered telling him that if they ever met again, it would be fate. Two months later, he again walked into my restaurant, and she remembered him well. He told her he believed it was his moment. They began talking, and she was more than happy to tell him her many problems. He took her to a house in an unfamiliar area. This house had no electricity, which means there was no heat, and no running water. She was very cold, so he bought her two pairs of jeans and a pair of boots. She slept in those boots and jeans every night. When she arrived at work every morning, she repeated the same routine of using a foam cup to cleanse herself over the toilet. She thought to herself, *I really need God himself to fix my situation.* That was when she began to pray. Her prayer was that he would turn things around for her. She was desperate!

There was a Cajun customer who frequented her restaurant. They never really spoke with each other, but one day, he brought two children along with him. His children did not appear clean. This caused her to become inquisitive, so she struck up a conversation. With their father's permission, she took them into the restroom and washed them up a bit. This was all too familiar to her. Washing up in the restroom had become the norm for her. She cooked them a meal and they talked.

He shared his troubles with her, as she shared hers with him. After she told him that she desperately needed a place to live, they started searching. Although she didn't have enough money, they searched every day on her break. This man was her angel sent from God. One day as they searched, she called out to a random stranger walking by and asked him if he knew where there might be places for rent. He replied, "I work for an apartment complex." Her friend made it clear to him that she would be moving in the apartment alone, but he obtained the apartment based on his own credentials.

"What a mighty God we serve!" God started opening other doors for her, and she was able to get a second job to pay my rent. Although God was opening doors for her, and although she was praying, she was a party girl at heart. She was always in the clubs, but she started focusing more on him. Even while focusing on God, she continued to frequent the night clubs, and went to church every now and then.

One night, while in the club; she looked at herself in the mirror. She was ugly! It was as if someone or something had transformed her into a ghostlike creature. She still had an illegal status but was blessed to get a new job, so she resigned from the restaurant. The job required her to work seven days per week, but she accepted it anyway. The same friend offered her a part-time job working every other weekend, and she accepted that as well. The full-time job required her to travel from one city to another every morning to work.

As if she needed more drama in my life, she became pregnant. She was not ready for the responsibilities of motherhood, especially single motherhood, so she considered an abortion. Although she had not made a total commitment to God, she felt guilty of even the thought of an abortion, but she made the appointment, arrived at the center and was prepped for the procedure.

Suddenly she heard the audible voice of her praying grandmother. She said, "If you go through with this abortion, you will die." She got up, got dressed, and left. She kept the baby, but as for his father, they went their separate ways. She decided that it would be easier to move to avoid so much traveling. She had ambitions of purchasing a home, but of course she couldn't do it in her own name, so she made the purchase in a friend's name. Not such a good idea. When her friend and she had an argument, the friend threatened to sell the house, and in the end that was exactly what she did. What an evil thing to do to someone, knowing she had no other options and a baby.

Still, she believed that God was setting her up. When the house was sold, she moved back again and started a business. Soon after, she bought her own house—yes, in her own name. She knew God was working on her heart, He was providing for her, and positioning her, but she couldn't stay away from the clubs. As Paul stated in Romans 7: The things that I didn't want to do are the things that I did. And the things that I wanted to do, I just couldn't do them.

One night while in the club, she became ill and knew she needed a change, so she asked her friend to go to church with her the next day, because she was tired of the life she was living.

The next day they went to church. She poured her heart out to God. She told him that she was tired of her current lifestyle. That day she could hardly wait for the altar call. The pastor's wife came to her seat and prayed with her. She took her to the altar. She was slain in the spirit and was on the floor for hours. She was saved and filled with the Holy Spirit. She received the gift of speaking in tongues that very day.

He was now her Lord, and he began to open more doors for her. Her business was doing well, and she had dreams of other businesses. If you are reading this story, never allow your dreams to slip away. We were all created with purpose, but if we are going to succeed, we must push past the difficulties.

This young woman became a prayer warrior. She wakes up early every morning and prays. She still does that today. Do you feel like you're being pushed? It may be uncomfortable, but don't complain, take a step of faith. It is God pushing you into your destiny. She went from living in a one-bedroom shack and multiple crack houses to her dream home. There were times when she felt hopeless, but today she's living the American dream. She married my son's father, and they had a second son. She thanks God every day for her amazing family.

She's gone from nothing to running six day care centers and one rental property. She is now a licensed real estate agent—a long way away from the $120 per week server position. It was extremely difficult, but she survived. Every time she fell, she was able to get back up again. She made it.

Just know beyond the shadow of a doubt that God works on the desires of your heart. Although we don't always live as we should, God provides for us and protects us. Never underestimate the power of prayer. Prayer is a powerful weapon of mass destruction. Her prayers destroyed poverty in her life. Prayer destroyed the yearning for the night clubs. He hears the heart before one uttered word. God himself pushed her into her purpose. The love of God filled every void and supplied everything she sought in those night clubs. She now pastors a church, and she prays for deliverance for all those who are seeking a better life, as she gives God the glory.

11

A Rose by Any Other Name: A Story of Survival and Intercession

The turkey was already seasoned and placed in the refrigerator to be cooked the next day, on Christmas Eve. Del had just made a pot of soup for a recovering cancer patient going through chemotherapy. That is when she received word that her grandson JJ had been in a car accident and was taken to an area hospital. Del herself had been taken to a different hospital on the evening before, complaining of headaches. Upon learning of JJ's accident, she insisted on accompanying her great-niece, JJ's sister, to the hospital. JJ's father was also notified, and he was on his way as well.

As Del entered the hospital emergency room, she collapsed. Just as she landed on the floor, her son, JJ's father, who is a veteran respiratory therapist technician, also entered the emergency room. He raced over to his mother as she lay lifeless on the hospital floor and administered mouth-to- to mouth resuscitation. Del had been misdiagnosed the night before; she had actually suffered a brain aneurism. That was going to be the longest three weeks of her family's lives.

The doctor, an Englishman, sat with the family and encouraged them to pray if they believed in prayer. Of course, that was all this family knew to do, so they tried to pray. During that time, Del's son-in-law, a pastor, encouraged her children to unite their hearts and pray as never before. Del's children were so distraught that they could not pray, but they sought help from everyone else who they thought knew the power of prayer. Del raised her children in church and spoke often of the many times God answered her prayers. Having this upbringing, they sent out calls to New York, Canada, Jamaica, and everywhere there was a praying person. Del remained in an induced coma as the doctor stented her brain.

One Saturday morning as the children sat in the hospital's surgical waiting room, the church evangelist called one of Del's daughters and asked a very significant question: "Are you willing to just sit there, or would you like to do something about this attack on your mother?"

Her daughter replied, "I don't know what to do, I am so scared."

The evangelist replied, "I am going to the church to pray for your mother." She did, and three weeks later, a miracle happened. Del opened her eyes. She was disoriented and weak and had to speak through a tube, but she was very much alive. She had weeks of therapy to regain her strength and mobility. Every therapist who treated her was amazed at her speedy recovery.

It has been ten years since Del suffered that aneurism. She is now eighty-three years old, very mobile, energetic, and independent. No one could have done this but God himself. It is imperative that we save up our praises, our worship and our prayers. The day may come when you can't pray for yourself. Never dismiss anyone; you never know who you'll draw from in your lifetime. Embrace your brothers and sisters. Love, forgive, and celebrate one another.

Our God is beyond awesome! He has made every provision for his people. He is the ultimate intercessor, and he wants us to intercede for one another. Intercessory prayer is the act of going to God on someone else's behalf. Intercession seeks God's glory, not our own. Intercessory prayer works. Del's case was a perfect example of how effective intercessory prayer is.

The Bible has given us many examples of intercessory prayers. There was the maid who interceded for Naaman, the man with leprosy. She gave him instructions on what to do for the leprosy to leave his body. Blind Bartimaeus was interceded for, so that he would get his sight. Then there were the ten lepers who were healed. Let's not forget about the woman with the issue of blood. When Peter was in jail, the women prayed, and he was released. Jesus told Peter that he himself prayed for him, so that the devil would not destroy him.

Don't ever be embarrassed if you have to ask someone to lift you up in prayer. Jesus remains at the right hand of God the Father making intercession for us. If you can't pray, God understands your groanings. If you need to, ask someone to intercede for you. God ordained intercession, so go ahead.

12

Weapons of Mass Destruction

———— ~❦~ ————

The weapons of our warfare are not carnal, but they are mighty through the pulling down of strongholds. There are two classes of weapons. One is carnal; the other spiritual. The carnal weapons include knives, guns, missiles, and bombs.

Spiritual weapons include the Word, which is the sword of the Spirit, prayer, praise, and worship (see Ephesians 6:17). As Christians, we must choose spiritual weapons. They work! God has given us the power of attorney to use his Word in any and every situation. No caveat is needed prior to using God's Word.

When David slew Goliath, it was not just the one smooth stone that killed Goliath. It was the word as well. In 1 Samuel 17:45 we read that David told Goliath, "You come to me with a sword, but I come to you in the name of the Lord of Hosts." Ironically, the name Jesus contains five letters, representing the five smooth stones that David chose. When Ezekiel needed to revive the dry bones, he commanded them to hear the word of the Lord (Ezekiel 37). The bones came back to life.

I join with the apostle John in chapter 1 of his gospel. There John states that the Word is alive. The Word is God himself. The scripture states: "In the beginning was the Word, The Word was God, and the Word was with God. The same God that was in the beginning at the creation." So you see, the Word is very much alive.

Prayer, the communication process that connects us to God is another of our weapons. Prayer is a solemn request for help or an expression of thanks to God. Prayer was the weapon that Jesus used when he called Lazarus from the dead. "Lazarus, come forth!"

The praying women used prayer when Peter was in jail. Prayer is such a powerful weapon that even when you can't open your mouth, God understands your groanings. The groanings have power. Haven't you been there, where situations got a hold of you and you just couldn't pray? We have all been there. Daniel prayed three times a day, every day (see Daniel 6:10). When Solomon completed the temple, he prayed as he dedicated the temple to God: "If my people who are called by name would humble themselves and pray, and seek my face, and turn from their wicked ways; then will I hear from heaven, I will forgive their sin and heal their land" (2 Chronicles 7:14).

Another weapon of warfare we often ignore as we are going through an attack is praise. Praise is given because of what God has done for us. "Let everything that hath breath praise the Lord." During this time, some, even Christians, give up or get discouraged. Some don't even want to go to church; and if they do, they just spectate. In Psalm 150, God calls upon everything to praise him:

Praise ye the Lord; Praise him in the sanctuary,
Praise Him in Firmament of his power.

Praise Him for His mighty acts. Praise Him
according to His excellent greatness.
Praise Him with the sound of the trumpet, praise
Him with the psaltery and harp.
Praise him with the timbral and dance, praise Him
with the stringed instruments and organ.
Praise Him upon the loud cymbals, Praise Him
upon the high-sounding cymbals.
Let every thing that hath breath praise the Lord.
Praise ye the Lord.

There are references in the Bible where praise is used as a weapon: In 2 Chronicles 20:21, Jehoshaphat used his praise team as a weapon. When he was about to do battle with the enemy, the praise team was placed at the front line of the battleground. I believe that was the first mention of a praise team. They of course won the battle.

In Joshua 6, a shout of praise brought down the walls of Jericho. Praise is a weapon of mass destruction—destruction of the enemy's plans. Some have asked, Can a sinner praise God? After all, the Bible does say praise is comely for the upright. Remember, the Bible states that everything that hath breath should praise the Lord. Yes! Everyone and everything should praise the Lord. To praise is to highly commend someone or express approval of them. You do not have to be a Christian to praise God.

Another Weapon Seldom Used Is Worship

Praise is for everyone and everything, but worship is for the saints. No matter what we are going through, we must continue to worship. Worship requires sacrifice, which is why worship is for

Christians. We don't worship because of how we feel, and we don't worship expecting anything in return. We worship because of who we know, and what we know. Worship is an upspringing of the heart that has known the Father as giver, the Son as a Savior, and the Holy Spirit as the indwelling power of God. When we worship, we just thank God for who he is. So then, can a sinner worship? A sinner does not know the son as Savior, so a sinner cannot yet worship.

So many people talk about it, but not many people know what true worship really is. Most of us sing really loud on Sunday, and people really believe that that is true worship. The apostle Paul really brings it home in Romans 12, when he states that we should present our bodies a living sacrifice holy and acceptable to God, our reasonable service. He goes on to remind us not to be conformed to this world but to be transformed by the renewing of our minds. We are not capable of worshiping the Lord God with a natural mind; the apostle Paul reminds us that we need a new mind in order to worship God.

Some of us are only motivated to worship when problems arise in our lives. We should wake up worshipping every morning. As one song writer puts it: "When I think of the goodness of Jesus and all He's done for me, my soul cries out Hallelujah! Thank God for saving me." If we are going to be delivered, we must use the weapons of mass destruction.

13

My Story ... His Glory!

―――――――― ⁓❧⁓ ――――――――

***Overcoming obstacles, challenges, and humble
beginnings so God can be glorified in our lives***

We all have a story. Our story is our testament to what has happened.
Our testament is our testimony ... also known as our story. I'm sure
that in our story, we can testify that in the most hurtful times, the
saddest times, when we thought we couldn't make it, we felt the very
presence of God at one point or another.

God Shows Up in Our Stories

He might have shown up through his word, the spoken Word of
God one Sunday. He might have shown up through one of his men
or women servants. When a phone call came at the very moment we
wanted to take our lives, God was there. That is our story.

Each Story Is Unique

Know that each person's story is different. There may be similarities, but God gives us unique experiences in this life. Sometimes it's a short story; other times it's a novel. But everyone has one. Your story I'm sure has ups and downs, twists and turns. Drama. Joy. Sadness. Possibly every emotion one could think of, right?

Definition of a Story

A story is an account of past events in someone's life; an account of incidents or events; widely circulated news or information. God has given all of us a story. There is value in stories. Stories tell others what happened. They have reference points that can be used to encourage, to uplift, to defeat, to restore, and to heal.

The Bible Broken Down into Stories

The Bible is all about stories. It is broken down for us in the Old Testament and the New Testament. And just in case we may have wondered what the purpose of this story was, God had that covered, when he said, "All scriptures are written for our edification. So, in essence, we need stories to be uplifted. To serve God. To know God." There is the story of Jesus (the greatest story ever told), the story of the creation, and stories of faith, of deliverance, of freedom, and of healing.

Elements of a Story

There are certain elements that make it a story. Here it is, broken down. There is the plot, the setting, the characters, the theme, the conflict (which includes the rising conflict, the climax, and falling conflict), and the resolution.

Plot:

Setting:

Characters:

Theme:

Theme Song:

Conflicts:

Resolution:

As a point of reference, movie creators, writers, and film directors create storyboards for their motion pictures. They take all of the elements of the story, organize them, and put them together. They do allow some room for the more seasoned actors to improvise off script. But they still have to come back on track in support of the theme and the desire pf the creator.

God, the Creator of the Universe

That is just like God. He has given each and every one of us a story wherein he is the Creator. He created the universe. He created mankind. But he didn't just speak it for us. He took time—went down in the cool of the day.

And he didn't just do it on His own. He said, "This is going to be a big one!" You see, he needed to make a beautiful creation, the most beautiful one yet. So, he called on the Holy Trinity. And as a result, God said, "Come, Let Us make man in our own Image!"

He scooped up dirt and put His own spit on it. Then he made man. As if that wasn't good enough, he put Adam to sleep, just to create Eve. He loved me so much that he made me out of the rib. He said it was not good for man to be alone. You see, when we are alone, we are too idle. Our thoughts start to race. No one man is an island. There is strength in numbers. So God made for Adam a wife. "For what God has joined together, let no man put asunder." That is why the enemy fights marriages so much. Because it is the greatest commitment outside of salvation that you can have on this earth.

He Formed Us in the Womb. "I Know the Plans I Have for You."

What is most interesting about life is that Jeremiah proclaims that before we were even formed in the womb, God knew us. In fact, he had predestined us. God's will is already being prepared for us. Granted, we have free will, but God said later in Jeremiah 29: I know the plans I have for you ... to prosper you and Give you a Bright hope and a future. So God had already known His desires for us. He had a plan. Just like that movie creator, the Creator of the universe has mapped out our storyboard, our destiny.

14

The Story of Ruth and Naomi

―――――― ～✿～ ――――――

Before I present Ruth chapter 4, I want to give you a brief summary of what happened in the first three chapters. There are so many themes and lessons in this story: loyalty, family bonds, faithfulness, love, endurance, trust, obedience, and faith.

Ruth Chapter 1

Ruth chapter 1 lays the foundation for what was going on.

Naomi was an older woman who was the mother-in-law to two women, Orpah and Ruth. And their story was that there was a famine in the land. After the deaths of her husband and her two sons, Naomi was in a depressed state. Nevertheless, she was concerned about her two daughters-in-law. She wanted them to remarry. She wanted them to move on with their lives. She cared for them. It wasn't a misery loves company scenario. She encouraged them to return home to their mothers. They didn't want to leave Naomi, but upon her insistence, Orpah left. Ruth stayed.

That is when Ruth uttered those famous words, "Entreat me not to leave thee"—meaning, please stop trying to get me to leave you. "Where you go, I will go. Where you lodge, I will lodge, where you die I want to die, where you are buried, I want to be buried. Your people will be my people and your God my God." She closed by saying only death would keep them apart.

So many people would have left. When the times are great, they celebrate with you. When tough times come upon you, they leave. We've all known people like those.

Naomi started to feel as though God had dealt harshly with her. She had lost her sons, she had lost her husband, and now one of her daughters-in-law, with whom she had a good relationship, had left. There was a famine. She felt old. She felt tired.

But Ruth stayed. Why? Because destiny had not yet been fulfilled. Because she loved Naomi. She respected her. They had that godly type of connection, wherein God said, I will never leave you nor forsake you.

Ruth bore the image of God. In tough times, God will be there. In sad times, he is there. Psalms indicates that when you soar into the heavens with wings like a dove, he is there. Even if you make your bed in hell, lo, I am there. Even when you walk through the valley of the shadow of death, yea I am with you ... my rod ... protection and my staff ... thy guide. They will comfort you.

Naomi's Return to Town: "Is That Naomi?"

Ruth was smart. I could only imagine how she sat back and watched Naomi function. Naomi was well known in the town, because the Bible says that when she returned, perhaps looking more tired and worn, the townswomen began asking among themselves, "Is that Naomi?"

Can you think of anyone like that? They hate on you and never give you a compliment when you're looking good, but when you start going through something, they notice? When you gain a few pounds, they not only notice, but they are happy to tell you.

She said, "I don't want to be referred to as Naomi, because the meaning of Naomi is 'pleasant.'

"Instead call me *Mara*, which means 'bitterness,' for I am bitter because God has dealt harshly with me. I went away full, but the Lord has brought me back empty. Why call me Naomi? The Lord has afflicted me; the Almighty has brought misfortune upon me."

But don't you know that all things work together for good? That is when God gets ready to do his best work ... when you are at your lowest!

Naomi's Worth ... We don't realize our worth

You see, during that period, although Naomi did not realize her worth, Ruth did. Similarly, at times, we can't realize our worth. The enemy uses that to keep us down. To keep us defeated.

Thank God for the Ruths in our lives who tell us we are beautiful. We are strong. We are able. We are loved.

Ruth had watched how Naomi cared for her husband. She had raised up good sons. She was aware of her family affairs; I'll tell you how this is demonstrated shortly. So she was a mentor and good example to Ruth.

Sometimes God puts people in your life who serve on this earth as guardian angels. We are to look to them as godly examples here on earth. Likewise, he also places women in our lives for us to lift up, to be mentors, prayer partners, and encouragers. Sometimes we fail to realize it! Sometimes because we've been hurt or betrayed, we automatically feel that someone else is going to hurt or betray us.

Ruth Chapter 2: In Walks Boaz—Destiny

In Ruth chapter 2 we're introduced to the man named Boaz. What I love about Ruth is that she wasn't lazy. She worked from dusk till dawn with a short break. She said, "Let me go into the field and pick up the leftovers for Naomi and myself." As she was busy working, she caught the eye of a young man named Boaz.

In walked destiny. Boaz started to ask about her, who's that woman? They workers told him about her.

"I have told the men not to lay a hand on you." He was getting ready to put his name on it. Or as we say today, put a ring on it. "And whenever you are thirsty, go and get a drink from the water jars the men have filled."

Boaz Heard About Ruth's Care for Naomi

Boaz replied, "I've been told all about what you have done for your mother-in-law since the death of your husband—how you left your father and mother and your homeland and came to live with a people you did not know before.

"May the Lord repay you for what you have done. May you be richly rewarded by the Lord, the God of Israel, under whose wings you have come to take refuge."

"May I continue to find favor in your eyes, my lord," she said. "You have put me at ease by speaking kindly to your servant." In other words, ladies … you know what she meant … I'm single, so put a ring on it!

At mealtime Boaz said to her, "Come over here. Have some bread and dip it in the wine vinegar."

When she sat down with the harvesters, he offered her some roasted grain. She ate all she wanted and had some left over.

As she got up to glean, Boaz gave orders to his men, "Let her gather among the harvested grain and don't reprimand her. Even pull out some stalks for her from the bundles and leave them for her to pick up, and don't rebuke her."

So Ruth gathered until evening. Then she threshed the barley she had gathered, and it amounted to about thirty pounds. She carried it back to town, and her mother-in-law saw how much she had gathered. Naomi asked her, "Where did you work? Blessed be the man who took notice of you!"

Then Ruth told her mother-in-law about the one at whose place she had been working. "The name of the man I worked with today is Boaz," she said. "He looked out for me and informed his workers to do the same."

You see, because she showed Naomi lovingkindness, God allowed her to receive it from Boaz. The Bible says blessed are the merciful, for they obtain mercy.

Ruth Chapter 3: Ruth Prepares to Lie at Boaz's Feet

Ruth's mother-in-law Naomi said to her, "My daughter, I must find a home for you, where you will be well provided for. Tonight, Boaz will be down by the mill where he is harvesting. Bathe, and put on perfume and your finest clothes.

"Don't reveal yourself just yet. Let him know you are there until he has finished eating and drinking. When he lies down, note the place where he is lying. Then go and uncover his feet and lie down. He will tell you what to do."

The critical point was that Ruth said, "I will do whatever you say." So in obedience, she did everything her mother-in-law and mentor told her to do.

When Boaz was finished eating and drinking and was in good spirits, he went over to lie down at the far end of the grain pile. Ruth approached quietly, uncovered his feet and lay down.

In the middle of the night something startled the man; he turned—and there was a woman lying at his feet! "Who are you?" he asked.

"I am your servant, Ruth," she said.

"The Lord bless you, my daughter," he replied. He didn't regard her as a stalker or weirdo because destiny was about to give birth. Divine providence was taking place. Instead, Boaz declared, "This kindness is greater than that which you showed earlier."

Boaz also noted that she did not chase after the younger men, whether rich or poor. "And now, my daughter, don't be afraid. I will do for you all you ask. All the people of my town know that you are a woman of noble character.

"Stay here for the night, and in the morning if your relative here wants to do his duty as your guardian-redeemer, good; let him redeem you. But if he is not willing, as surely as the Lord lives I will do it. Lie here until morning."

So, she lay at his feet until morning, but got up before anyone could be recognized; and he said, "No one must know that a woman came to the threshing floor." God's glory covered her.

He also said, "Bring me the shawl you are wearing and hold it out." When she did so, he poured into it six measures of barley and placed the bundle on her. Then he went back to town.

When Ruth came to her mother-in-law, Naomi asked, "How did it go, my daughter?"

Then she told her everything Boaz had done for her and added, "He gave me these six measures of barley, saying, "Don't go back to your mother-in-law empty-handed."

Conclusion: Ruth and Boaz Conceive

It didn't end there. I'm going to summarize it for you. In Ruth chapter 4, the Bible talks about how Boaz bought up the land, and he also married Ruth.

God's glory is about to manifest. And Boaz, Ruth, Naomi, and generations to come—including you and me—are about to experience the glory.

God Enables Conception

The Word of God says that after Ruth and Boaz married, *the Lord allowed her to conceive a son.* That leads me to be believe that since she had no children prior to this, she was not able to conceive with her first husband.

God enables conception ….

Natural Conception

So Ruth gave birth to a son named Obed.

In the last two years, I have researched a lot about conception. First of all, I knew that it takes a womb or uterus. It also takes an ovum or egg and the seed (from the man).

All pieces of the process must work together. What I learned recently was that there is only one time per month that a woman is able to conceive. No matter how many eggs she has, no matter how much seed is present, they must work together in sync.

For the woman to conceive, she needs the seed. She can't do it without it.

Ruth is our example today. She knew the season that she was in: a season of famine, a season of mourning. She also understood that weeping may endure for a night, but joy was coming.

She didn't stay in the place that she was in. She had to get up and move because faith without works is dead. She exercised *obedience*—to Naomi and to Boaz ... ultimately to God. She also lifted her faith!

Because of faith and obedience, she conceived her blessing. So Ruth gave birth to Obed.

Obed is a boy's name and is of Hebrew origin, and the meaning of Obed is "servant of God; worshipper, follower." Obed was the father of Jesse, and Jesse the father of King David. The lineage continues all the way until you get to our Savior, Jesus Christ.

The Bible says that Naomi took this baby boy and cradled him in her arms. And the women said, "He will renew your life and sustain you in your old age."

It was probably the same women who were talking about her two chapters ago.

Thou preparest a table before me in the presence of mine enemies!

Obedience and Faith Are Conceived into Destiny

Ruth exercised obedience and faith to get to destiny.

You who have been blessed to read this book, if you are seeking a mighty move of God in this season for greater, for more, for better, for higher, for deeper, ask God to enlarge your territory.

God wants us to birth a deeper worship. Salvation for our children. A ministry, a preacher. Healing, that family member on drugs, gender identity confusion. A preacher. A ministry. Healing.

Where two or three are gathered, he is in the midst!

He wants to enable us to conceive and birth a business. Birth healing. Birth a home. Birth a renewed marriage. Deliverance. Our dreams. Our hopes. What are you trusting God for today?

In understanding my own fertility, my doctors taught me a lot that I didn't know before. A lot goes into conception, believe it or not. There is typically one day per month that you can conceive. But so much goes into planning it when you're actively trying.

Conception: Temperature Rising—Egg and Seed

Leading up to conception, your body temperature (they call it your basal body temperature) increases. Doctors say you can chart your ovulation by your temperature. It is at its highest just before your chances of conception are greatest.

The battle is the hottest, just before victory! The tempest rages the most before the calm comes! The fire is the hottest before pure gold.

But God promises, when you go through the fire, you shall not be burned. It's not even going to scorch you!

You're coming out as pure gold!

You're coming out with your story!

You're coming out with purpose!

You're coming out for God's glory!

So, then the *ovum* and *seed* must unite. The two must meet and come in contact with the uterus for conception to take place.

Then at the appointed day and appointed time, the birthing process begins.

I want to encourage you that if I had to make a reference, think of the ovum as obedience. Ruth was obedient. She didn't squabble or put up a fuss. She let go and let God.

Faith is the seed that had to meet up with obedience. Faith is the substance of things hoped for and the evidence of things not seen. Without faith it is impossible to please God.

The Ovum = Obedience.

The Seed = Faith. If you have faith the size of a mustard *seed*, you can move mountains!

They connected and conceived in destiny.

The Womb = Destiny.

> For whom he did foreknow, he did predestinate.
> And whom he predestinated, he justified.
> And whom he justified, he glorified.
> What shall we say to these things? If God be for us,
> then who can be against us?

All for the glory of God to reign supreme in our lives and so that we can share our story of God's glory with others.

Inside of the womb, you need blood. You also need fluid for nutrients for the unborn.

The Nutrients found within the placenta = Grace, Love, Forgiveness, Mercy, and Favor

The Blood is necessary. The Blood is the life. The Blood is the Blood of Jesus. The Blood that Jesus shed way back on Calvary shall never lose its power.

For it reaches to the highest mountain. It flows to the lowest valley.

The blood that gives me strength from day to day shall never lose its power.

Hallelujah!

The process started. So, as you are about to conceive your blessing from God, just know that things might get hot, but God is in control.

Decree and declare in this season of grace upon your life, that God is going to enable you to conceive in the Spirit.

If you believe, you can conceive. If you conceive, you will achieve!

If you know that God will bring it to pass, then take some time and praise Him for what he's about to do. Give God the glory; it belongs to him.

15

Hold On Till He Blesses You

———— ❧ ————

I don't know about you, but I am counting my blessings! Just this week, I was thanking God for all that he has done. Just when I thought He already did so much for me, Jesus did it again!

I speak to your very hearts for the next few minutes, and I pray that we will hear, as thus says the Lord of Hosts.

Genesis chapter 32 tells us about a man named Jacob. I will give you some background about him.

Esau was a hunter, what we would call an "outdoorsman." As he returned from a hunting trip one day, he saw Jacob cooking some stew. Jacob offered Esau a bowl of it in exchange for Esau's birthright as the oldest son. Esau despised his birthright and gave it to Jacob in exchange for a bowl of stew. Moody said, "No food except the forbidden fruit was as [expensive] as this broth." Esau wanted to gratify his physical appetite, and so he lost the spiritual blessing for him and his descendants.

Several years passed. Isaac was now very old and very blind. He called Esau to him and asked him to go and kill a deer and make him savory venison that he loved to eat. As Esau went hunting, Jacob's

83

mother cooked goat's meat and made it taste like venison. Jacob took the meat to his father and pretended to be Esau. He fooled his blind, old father, and Isaac blessed Jacob, thinking he was Esau. The blessing was prophetic and literally came to pass, because Isaac spoke by inspiration.

When Esau returned from hunting, he learned that Jacob had tricked him out of his birthright. Esau sought this blessing as well, but it was too late. The Book of Hebrews says,

> Lest there be any fornicator, or profane person, as Esau, who for one morsel of meat sold his birthright. For ye know how that afterward, when he would have inherited the blessing, he was rejected: for he found no place of repentance, though he sought it carefully with tears. (Hebrews 12:16–17)

Notice that Esau sought the inheritance and the blessing, but he did not seek God. He sought "it" carefully, but he did not seek God. He sought "the blessing" with tears, but he never sought for God. You see, Esau never thought about God. God was not in his thoughts. And so God said, "Jacob have I loved, but Esau have I hated" (Romans 9:13).

That was his failing. Esau never thought about God! *Esau never once mentioned God in the Book of Genesis.* Think of it; Esau was born and raised in the home of the patriarch Isaac—and yet *he never mentioned the name of God.*

Jacob Meets Esau

So the hope of Jacob was that he would be blessed with Esau's forgiveness. Esau would soften his heart and withdraw his death threats or promises. He had even been told that Esau was on the way and was bringing hundreds of men. Just imagine how Jacob must have been deathly afraid. Plus he had his wives and children. In those days, if the head was killed, it was not unheard of to either kill everyone else or take them as slaves. So Jacob needed intervention.

Genesis 32:22–31

I am always encouraged when I read Genesis 32: 22–31, because I know that Jacob was an imperfect man. He made mistakes. He lied. He was tricky. But he acknowledged God. He loved God. He sought after his blessing.

What I love most is how the scripture references how he got his blessing. It's a model for us to follow. He wrestled for his blessing.

Just to be clear, we don't have to wrestle God for our blessing, because he desires to bless us. We figuratively use wrestling today as a means to demonstrate that we are not going to let go, not going to give up … until we are victorious.

We are more than conquerors!

Do you need a blessing from the Lord today? Some of us are wrestling right now. But I am here to encourage you: Don't give up. Hold on to your marriage. Hold on to that job you know God promised. Hold on to what the Lord has promised. Don't let go until you get your breakthrough.

I love the Bible's use of the term *wrestling*. Genesis 32 uses this term to define Jacob's journey to his blessing in the Old Testament.

We no longer have physical encounters like these. In the New Testament, Ephesians reminds us of that. Ephesians 6:12 starts out to say that we wrestle not against flesh and blood ….

I, for one, would probably lose if I had to physically wrestle for my blessing. Many of us would not be blessed if that were the case. Especially after a big meal … you know how we get!

However, let me enlighten you today that, like Jacob, if you hold on and don't let go, you will receive your blessing.

Since the action word in this text is *wrestle*, we're going to stay right there.

For those of you who are wrestling fans, like me when I was younger, I loved wrestling.

Are You a Wrestler?

One definition of wrestling is that it is a contact sport. A wrestling bout is a physical competition, between two (occasionally more) competitors or sparring partners, who attempt to gain and maintain a <u>superior position</u>.

What I remembered about wrestlers years ago is that each wrestler had a signature name and a signature move. These signature moves is what got them to the goal, which was to overcome and win.

Well must like those wrestlers, we are spiritual wrestlers today. And sometimes, there are those things in this life- blessings that we need, that we will have to put extra moves into- in order to overcome and win.

I will give you four wrestling moves that will help you as they have helped me.

#1: Acknowledge God. Young people, develop a life of recognizing God. Start by saying something nice about him. You're awesome. You're wonderful. You're supreme. You're merciful. Recognize that the Creator of the universe is awesome. Thank him for sending his Son, Jesus.

#2: Faith. Faith without works is dead. If we have faith the size of a mustard seed, the Bible says we can move any mountain. The

Bible also says that we walk by faith and not by sight. So get your faith walk together. Perfect it. After Jacob was hit in his hip, the Bible said that he limped ever since.

#3: Pray. Develop your prayer. It doesn't even have to be long and drawn out. The Bible says that the prayer of the righteous availeth much.

There was a young man by the name of Jabez in 1 Chronicles 4:9–10. His mother named him because of the pain she had in his birth. Jabez looked around and saw the generational curses that had befallen his family, and he said, "Oh that you would bless me indeed, and enlarge my territory." *Indeed* indicated a right now need. He put emphasis on it. The Bible says that God answered his request.

Do you need your territory enlarged today? In business? In relationships? In your marriage? In education? In ministry? What do you need from the Lord? Ask him to bless you *indeed*.

#4: Praise him. Let everything that hath breath praise the Lord. On the instruments. Lift your hands. Grab your tambourines and praise him. Wars were won with praise. When Jehoshaphat went to war, God told him to stand still, get his praise and worship team together, and put them on the front line. They began to praise God. The enemy became confused and fought and killed each other. That's the God that we serve.

When Paul and Silas were in prison, the Bible says that as they prayed at midnight, the prison walls shook. The jailer was so moved that he gave his life to the Lord.

In Closing

I just want to remind you today, just like Jacob, don't let go of your blessing! Don't give up! Don't give in. Sometimes circumstances make it look like it's not going to happen.

But don't give up. Get your wrestling moves together.

Acknowledge the One who lay in the grave for three days and got up with all power in his hand. Walk by faith.

Pray, for when we ask, we shall receive the promises of God.

Praise Him; God doesn't need our praise—he deserves it.

As I close, just like Jacob, declare a new name. My name is blessed. My name is delivered. My name is healed. My name is minister. My name is mommy. My name is wife. My name is committed. Whatever it is that you need from God, claim it right now.

Begin to call those things that are not as though they are. Hold on for your blessing! Watch God move on your behalf! May God bless you.

16

His Blood, My Liquid Glory

———— ✺ ————

There is power in the blood of Jesus. "For this is my blood of the New Testament, which is shed for many, for the remission of sins" (Matthew 26:28). Blood is the life of all flesh. Life is contained in the blood.

The word *blood* is mentioned many times throughout the Bible. The first mention that comes to mind is in Genesis 4:1–10, where the two sons of Adam, Cain and Abel, set out to offer sacrifices to God. The Lord God respected and accepted Abel's sacrifice but did not accept Cain's. Cain was of course very angry, and his countenance changed when he realized his sacrifice was unacceptable. Cain lured his brother out into the field, and there he killed him.

When God confronted Cain and asked after his brother, he replied, "I don't know. Am I my brother's keeper?"

God asked him, "What have you done? Your brother's blood cries out of the ground."

So you see, blood plays a significant role in the Bible and in our lives. When Canaan suffered a famine, Jacob and seventy others went down to Egypt. They settled in Goshen, and over time, the seventy multiplied into a great multitude. Some years after, this great multitude became enslaved by the reigning Pharaoh. They cried out to God, whose name they did not even know, but God heard their voice. One of the Hebrews, whose name was Moses, was raised by Pharaoh's daughter. When Moses was about forty years old, he killed two Egyptians who were abusing some of the enslaved Israelites. He then escaped to the country of Midian. That is where Moses met and married his wife.

One day while tending his father-in-law's sheep, he was led to Mount Horeb. While on Mount Horeb, Moses met God. God sent Moses back to the very place from which he'd run away. Isn't that just like God? His commission was to go back to deliver the enslaved Israelites. God is a deliverer! After negotiating with God, Moses finally accepted the commission.

God wrought many signs and wonders through Moses to get Pharaoh's attention, but nothing worked. Finally God hardened the heart of the enslaver, Pharaoh. In my opinion, God wanted to prove himself to his people. Here comes "Liquid Glory." Then as a final sign, God commanded Moses to have each family kill a young lamb. The blood of the lamb should be painted on the doorpost of their homes. That was and is still known as "Passover." The Israelites were told to eat standing and remain fully dressed.

That night, when the destroyer passed through, he killed all the firstborn Egyptians, both mankind and beast. When he saw the blood on the doorposts of God's people, he passed over them as promised. If the blood of the lamb was so significant, how much more is the blood of Jesus. If the blood of Abel cried out from the ground, how much more does the blood of Jesus cry out for the people he loves?

Matthew 26:28 states, "For this is my blood of the New Testament which was shed." "It was shed for many, for the remission of sins." The blood purchased the church. Acts 20:28 states: "Be shepherds of the church of God, which he bought with his own blood." His blood reaches all the way to the White House. It flows as low as the crack house.

On Good Friday the blood of Jesus flowed from his head, his hands, his feet. The first New Testament convert shouted out, "Lord when thou comest into thy kingdom, remember me!" The one whose blood flowed answered, "Today thou shalt be with me in Paradise!" The blood of Jesus washes away sin. Many song writers have written songs about the power in the name of Jesus. Hence the song: "The dying thief rejoiced to see that fountain in his day, and there may I though vile as he, wash all my sins away."

The blood of Jesus brings reconciliation (Colossians 1:20). I served in the Jamaica Defense Force, Army Division, for thirty years. While serving, I was a member of the Soldiers Prayer Group. The group met during lunch to praise, pray, and worship God.

One day I was asked to speak to the soldiers. In the midst was a lieutenant colonel. I shared a thought with the group: "Even if there were steps to Calvary, where the cross was lifted up was a level place." I also reminded the soldiers that we all will have to get to that level place—that place where blood and water ran from Jesus Christ and settled. Before I could complete the sermon, this high-ranking officer rose up and gave his life to the Lord. Today he is a well-renowned minister of the gospel. He is traveling all over the world and ministering the gospel.

The blood of Jesus replaced the previous sacrifices. The blood of Jesus paid the debt we owe. It forgives; it draws us close to God because it justifies and forgives. The blood of Jesus redeems us. It makes us alive. We were all dead in our trespasses and sins. The blood now allows us to enter the "Holy of Holies" (Hebrews 10:19). The blood of Jesus has replaced all other bloods.

The Bible tells us that Jesus was the lamb slain from the foundation of the world. It is clear then that God made provisions for us in advance. He anticipated all of our mistakes and imperfections. God knew about that illness and that abuse and that rape, and yes!—he knew you would be bullied. He sought you anyway. He knew about it before it happened, so he made the provision for it all before the problem. God's Word said, "I know the plans I have for you. Plans to prosper you, not to harm. Plans give you hope and a future." I hope and trust that as you read this book with all the various testimonies, if you are not saved, I encourage you to open your hearts and let the blood of Jesus wash you and make you clean.

Let go of all that has hurt you, because God made provision in advance for your victory. He died for it all. His blood, your liquid glory.

Printed in the United States
by Baker & Taylor Publisher Services